What people a
Freedom F.

I thoroughly enjoyed Freedom From Fear. It's a compelling story with plenty of great life lessons. I am convicted to invest more time each day for personal reflection and to read.
Robbo Newcomb, CEO,
Newcomb & Co.

Read this book from start to finish, preferably in one sitting. It's like having Mark Matteson next to you reading the story aloud. He is a great storyteller.
Randy Dec, Division Manager,
Lakeside Industries

I am amazed at how rich and meaningful the story is. Just a wonderful piece of work.
Scott Forslund, Director of Public Relations,
Premera Blue Cross

Freedom From Fear *reminded me of many powerful truths that I had lost sight of. I was inspired to return to practicing the ideas that the central character, Len, shared with others in the story. I couldn't put it down!*
Andrew Bennett,
Bennett Performance Group

Freedom From Fear *is a powerful modern day parable, a must read for anyone who wishes to live life more fully and in turn pass that wisdom on to others. Practice Len's Lessons and you will be at peace with your personal, professional and spiritual life.*
Alex Carney, Publisher,
Contracting Business Magazine

This story carries a great message for the young and old alike.
Armond Pearson, Founder and CEO,
Sleep Aire Mattress Company

MARK MATTESON

Freedom
F^{ROM}ear

The story of one
man's discovery of
simple truths that
lead to wealth, joy
and peace of mind

Freedom FROM Fear

Published by
Ugly Dog Publishing
206-697-0454
www.SparkingSuccess.net

ISBN: 978-0-9995350-0-4

LCCN: 2002102666

Printed in the United States of America

Table of Contents

Chapter 1

"Why Worry..."

It was raining hard the morning 2,000 people showed up to his funeral. Denny Park was a small church in a big city. In fact, it was the oldest church in the city, 1894. None of us in attendance could have imagined this many people would come to Seattle to honor a man that seemingly lived such a private life. I had no idea he even knew this many people! It was unbelievable. They were jammed into the church standing room only. What was really amazing was that I knew none of these people, not a single one. I silently hoped I would find out why. What was it that bound us all? Was his reach and influence really this broad? Had he affected this many lives? The sheer number of people he had apparently touched was incredible. I wondered silently if he had struck the same bargain with all these people that he had with me.

He was a coach. Not in athletic terms, but in *Life* Terms. He was the best coach I ever had. His classroom was the coffee shop. There was no doubt he was a unique man.

He used to say, "Freedom from fear is more important than freedom from want." What the heck did that mean? I didn't understand it at the time. He had these quotes, these maxims or proverbs that I had never heard before. They appeared just when I needed them the most. Once I got to know him I came to learn they were as much a part of him as his smile or the twinkle in his eye. He was always happy, always upbeat. I was jealous. I wanted what he seemed to have... laughter, joy, peace of mind, abundance.

*   *   *   *   *   *   *   *   *

It was 1979, I was 22 years old, just a puppy with a lot of drive. For ten years I had struggled with doubt, fear, insecurity, low esteem, no self-respect, though I managed to maintain a façade with the help of false humor and isolation.

Put on a good show, and as long as I kept people at a distance, as long as no one knew the real me, maybe they wouldn't suspect how I really felt inside: miserable. Oh yes, I also had this little problem with drugs and alcohol. I started drinking when I was 12 years old—I'll spare the long explanation as to why. Let's just say when I took that first drink, all those problems went away... temporarily. I came from a long line of alcoholics on both sides of my family. It was, at least to me, very natural to drink. Everyone I knew drank. My family, my friends in the neighborhood, their parents all drank with regularity.

Come to think of it, I can't remember anyone that didn't drink. So I grew up with the natural effects of that environment:

- I had very little Self-Confidence. When I would attempt a task with my father, the first mistake I made, he would snatch the tool out of my hands and say, "Let me do that, you're going too slow!" or "You're not doing that right!" I was like a dog that had been hit too many times, waiting for the shoe to drop.

- I was never required to finish what I started. That had a crippling effect on my Self-Respect and Esteem. I never knew what it meant to have positive feelings of accomplishment that come from sticking to the task until it's done. The message I received growing up, from stories, example and implicit message, was "it's okay to quit."

- Moderation?! What was that? All or nothing. More is better. Those maxims were what I learned and adopted as my own from the modeling all around me.

- Negative Self Talk. "What's the matter with me anyway?" "How could I be so stupid?" "Why does this kinda stuff always happen to me?" "I don't deserve good things." I thought this was normal.

- Pessimism. Blame, Complain, and Explain.

Everyone I knew played that game. If at first you don't succeed, set the blame quick. It's always the other guy's fault. If it wasn't for the Government, the teachers or coaches, the economy, this lousy boss of mine, my classmates or teammates, we would be doing much better.

- Dishonesty. I remember the first time I did something I wasn't supposed to do and told the truth. I got a spanking! I remember at five years old thinking, "The truth sure hurts." Then a week later, I did something again that I knew was wrong. Remembering the pain of truth telling, I did the most logical thing I could think of to avoid the pain... I lied. *It worked!* I didn't get in trouble. It was so easy. So painless. That day, I became a liar. "Oh what a tangled web we weave when first we practice to deceive," wrote Shakespeare. Years later my wife said something profound: "If you tell the truth, you don't have to remember what you said." I was working waaaay too hard.

- Resentment. How quickly I learned how to resent anyone that got in the way of anything I wanted. People, Institutions, Places, anything or anyone that hindered my quest for self-gratification was a candidate for my criticism and judgment. The sad part of this is I didn't just resent them once and let it go. I would harbor and nurse these resentments for weeks, months, years. Resentment, you see, comes from the Latin "Re," to repeat, and "Sentere," to feel. Sometimes juggling dozens of them at once, replaying them in my mind with all the old emotions of self-pity, revenge, anger and hostility over and over again like a broken record.

- Self-pity and Withdrawal. Over time, I learned to withdraw from people using whatever distraction seemed most useful or convenient at the time: food, TV, sleep, eventually alcohol and drugs. Isolation. Always alone in my thoughts and feelings. "Don't let 'em see you sweat." "Real men don't cry!" "Don't give me that soft and squishy crap." Those were the John Wayne messages I heard growing up. So guess what? I kept it all in. Sharing was for sissies. Talking about your feelings just wasn't done.

These and more were the very things I would have to unlearn. They represented the barriers to my own personal growth. I was emotionally and spiritually stunted. In retrospect, they were coping mechanisms that I picked up along the way. Abraham Maslow, the great industrial psychologist, once remarked, "If the only tool you know how to use is a hammer, all your problems look like nails."

So that is where I found myself after ten years of abstinence from spirits, from 1979 to 1989. But just not drinking wasn't enough: I was miserable.

It was a hot, humid summer day, and five o'clock traffic was at a snail's pace coming over the bridge. I only looked down for a moment. It had been one of those days. Nothing had gone right. I was listening to a blues tape and reading the liner notes when they fell to the floor of the car. That's when I ran into this guy. If you've ever been in an accident, you know the feeling: Sick to your stomach, a bottomless pit in your abdomen. "Great, just great," I thought. When you rear end someone, it's almost always your fault. How could I get out of this one?

He was a big bear of a man, 6'3" and 230 pounds, solid. He appeared to be in his mid 50s and had a wiry crop of grayish brown hair, like a robin's nest, a little uneven and out of place. The first thing he said to me was, "Are you all right?" He said it in such a kind and caring way, I was taken aback. "Yeah, I'm okay," I remarked in a sarcastic and negative tone. I was going to go into a long diatribe about why he had stopped so suddenly when he interrupted my thoughts with "Are you sure? You look kind of shook up." Now feeling a little guilty and foolish, I said, "Really, I'm all right. I'm sorry I ran into you, I sure didn't mean to." He smiled. "I understand how you feel, been there before myself," this stranger said to me calmly. There was an air about him, a manner quite disarming and comforting. We walked over to examine the damage. My car's bumper hit his bumper and, as they were the same height, no apparent damage had been done. "It doesn't appear as if there is any real damage, except for how bad you must be feeling. Do we need to call the police or are you okay with shaking hands and parting friends?" he asked me warmly. "No use getting the insurance companies involved if we don't have to." I paused for a moment relieved. That was music to my ears. "I would just as soon keep it between ourselves and I would be happy to pay any damages if you get home and find anything we missed," I said nervously.

"Here's my card," he said smiling. "Len is my name. And you are...?" Hesitating, I said, "Steve," and held out my hand to shake his. He had huge hands and a powerful grip. He shook my hand with enthusiasm and strength. At that moment I felt like we had met before. In the span of 20 seconds and a warm handshake, all my fear about the situation vanished and I felt at ease, calm and comforted. It was a strange and disarming effect. Who was this guy? "Nothing happens by accident. We were supposed to meet. Have a safe trip home. Be careful," Len said with compassion. "I will, thank you," I replied gratefully.

Driving away from this encounter I remember thinking, what a great guy. He could have been really nasty about it. Come to think of it, I had been in the same situation years before when someone hit my bumper and I was less than kind. Wow. I had no idea my life was about to change in a profound, meaningful and permanent way.

A day later, my phone rang. It was Len. "Do you remember me? We ran into each other yesterday on the bridge. I just wanted to see if you were okay. I also wanted to get your address. I'd like to send you something in the mail." Had it been almost anyone else, I would have felt suspicious or threatened. Somehow, though, I knew it was in my best interest to give him my PO Box. A few days later I received a little card with a quote on it. The quote said:

To live without FEAR is one of life's chief aims.

How strange he would send that. Yet it was exactly what I needed to hear at that moment. His card was in it so I called him. He agreed to meet me for lunch. I wanted to thank him for being so kind and to find out more about what made this guy tick.

In retrospect, it's clear to me I had been searching for a mentor for a long time. He was different than anyone I had ever met and he had what I was looking for. He seemed to have an abundance of peace of mind, confidence and joy. But most of all, he was genuine. He possessed humility. I didn't know I wanted that last quality. "Humility," he said to me years later, "is an interesting thing. The moment you think you have it, it's gone."

He was quiet most of the time. I envied that. For the first year I knew him I never knew his last name or what he did for a living. In conversation, he always dominated the listening. When he finally would speak, he commanded the attention of everyone. He always knew just what to say. He told a lot of stories. Sometimes they were funny, other times very sad. I learned later that, although he had gone to college on a sports scholarship, and although he had a degree in business, he was, for the most part, self-taught. Like me, he had two boys, and had been married to the same woman for 25 years when we met.

When I would call him, his answering service always played a different inspirational or thought provoking quote. Each week he picked a theme and, for seven days, the quote of the day related to that week's theme—a theme that was related to what he was teaching me. "Repetition is the mother of skill," he occasionally said. As he shared an insight, he could always tell when I was way out of my comfort zone and couldn't see how I was going to apply it. "What would people think?" I asked him one day. "Steve," he said, *"You wouldn't worry quite so much about what other people thought of you if you only realized how little they did."* That was my thought for the day. He had a new thought for me almost daily. I didn't know much back then but I was just dumb enough, just ready enough, just trusting enough to write them down.

"Most people are caught up in their own problems, they don't have the time or desire to worry about yours.

We all fall into the trap of obsessing about future events or feeling guilty about the past. You are going to learn to let that kind of thinking go. I'm out of time, let's meet again next week. But I want you to remember this—in fact, why don't you write this down:"

How important is this, really?

"It's easy to become complacent in our thinking and not pay attention to our thoughts, the words we use. We form habits of thinking and speaking without giving serious consideration to the effect they might have on how we feel. *First we form habits, then they form us.*" Whenever Len made a powerful point, he lowered his voice and, judging by his tone, this was one of those nuggets to remember. He continued, *"Good habits are hard to form and easy to live with. Bad habits are easy to form and hard to live with. If we don't consciously form good habits, we will unconsciously form bad ones. Pay attention. Be aware. Words are tools, they are neither true nor false until they become habitual and affect how we feel. Use them carefully. Monitoring your thoughts, your language, is one of the most difficult habits to form. It takes time.*

"Have you ever heard of *The Strangest Secret in the World?*" Len asked. "No," I replied. I remember feeling excited that this would be IT. The magic formula for success: it was coming. He smiled and leaned forward to tell me. I leaned forward to hear it. He whispered, *"We become what we think about."*

"What do you think about most of the time?" Len asked. "There is a real power in being aware. I have found through study, trial and error, and by paying attention—really listening to other people's self-talk first, my own thoughts and the words I use second—that much of my habitual thinking was, and *is,* erroneous. I adopted, albeit unconsciously, the habits and thought patterns of the people I spent the most time with growing up. When you're a kid, you don't give much consideration to this kind of thinking. Much of this I had to learn on my own. A great deal of what works for me I had to find out the hard way, trial and error, painful lessons captured and analyzed. Unlearning old habits is the key. Over time I will share the ideas, thoughts, principles and practices that have allowed me to enjoy the truly great things in life.

Along the way, I began doing more of what worked and less of what didn't until I formed the habits of happy and successful people. Introspection, reflection is a great tool for growth. I have found writing down my fears loosens their grip on me. When I write down my worries, and then share them with someone else, I cut them in half. It doesn't make sense to worry. It's a misuse of the imagination.

Len had a humorous bit of doggerel on his desk that said,

Why Worry?

There are only two things to worry about...
Either you are sick or you are well.
If you are well, then there is nothing to worry about.
But if you are sick, there are only two things to worry about...
Either you will get well or will die.
If you get well there is nothing to worry about.
But if you die, there are only two things to worry about...
Either you go to heaven or to hell.
If you go to heaven, there is nothing to worry about.
If you go to hell...
you'll be so busy shaking hands with old friends, you
won't have time to worry! ☺

Failing to see the humor, I said, "This is all well and good, Len, but you don't have the problems I do. I'm feeling bad right now. Nothing is going right. My job stinks, my wife won't listen to me, my boss is always on my case." I felt like I was at confessional, talking with a priest.

"How long is this going to be a problem?" Len asked in a very calm and relaxed tone. "One minute, hour, day, week, month? No one can do this for you. I have found the harder I work on me, the better my life goes. When I commit to my own personal development and stick with it, the better my life goes, the more money I make, the better I get along with the people I work with, with my family. It's amazingly simple. If it's to be, it's up to me."

Smiling, he continued, "Do you know what FEAR is, really? It's an acronym. F.E.A.R. means *False Evidence Appearing Real*. It's an illusion. Listen, I have got to run. Let's meet next Saturday, same time?"

"Yes that would be great," I said, a little numb. Then he was gone. I reached for a napkin and wrote down everything I could remember about our conversation.

Len's Lessons

Napkin Notes on thoughts that occurred to me while I was listening, and quotes that made me think…

"You wouldn't worry quite so much about what other people thought of you if you only realized how little they actually did!"

"We become what we think about."

"How important is this, really? What is the worst thing that would happen if the thing I am worrying about came true?"

"Good habits are hard to form and easy to live with. Bad habits are easy to form and hard to live with. Pay attention. Be aware. If we don't consciously form good ones, we will unconsciously form bad ones."

"If I put my problems on paper and then share them with someone that cares, I cut them in half. Conversely, if I share my joys I double them."

"How long will I let this issue be a challenge? How long will I let fear, resentment or self pity consume me, one minute, one hour, one Day, one Week, one Month? It's up to me to change my mind, no one else can do that for me!"

"First we form habits, then they form us."

"To live without fear is one of life's chief aims."

Chapter 2

"Readers Read"

John was sitting next to me at Len's funeral. He was an average looking guy, in his mid-forties, blond hair, slightly balding, and kind of heavy set. He didn't look like a millionaire. I asked him, "How did you know Len?" He said, "Len helped me at a time when I was down and out. Not a dime to my name. I had lost everything on Black October, the stock market crash of 1987, but mostly I lost my self-respect and dignity." He was a stockbroker that had bet it all on pork bellies and oranges and lost. Len had helped him earn it back. In the ten years since he met Len, he had become wealthy in the dry cleaning business on the East Coast. He shared his story...

"Len taught me so many things. But the most profound and meaningful things I learned were what I observed of him when we were together. For instance, I noticed that every time we met, he always had a book with him. Invariably, if we agreed to meet somewhere, he was always there early and was lost in a book. It was a different book every time: business, leadership, biography, classic literature, self-help, spiritual, economics, poetry. His interests were broad and varied. Ever present, next to the book, his journal. He was a true student. When I commented on that, he said, *'The books you don't read won't help. People who don't read are no better off than those who don't know how to read.'"*

As John told his story, I remembered something Len said to me so many years ago: "Be a student not a follower. If someone recommends a book to you, by all means read it. Then read two or three other books on the same subject and make up your own mind. Let your beliefs and philosophy become the product of your own conclusion. Avoid being a cynic. Learn to become a healthy skeptic until you've done your homework. I've found that to be best."

Catching myself not paying strict attention, almost as if I was in a black and white flashback in a color movie, I came back to listening about John's experience with Len. "He used to say to me, 'You'll be the same person in five years as you are today with the exception of two things: the people you associate with and the books that you read.'" As John said that, I reflected back on the hundreds of books I had read and the countless new friendships that I formed as a result of the learning, and smiled. He was right. I am so different in just five short years as a result of my commitment to learning, growth and realizing my own personal greatness.

John continued, "One of the curious aspects of the dynamic of growth and personal development is the subtle migration away from others who are not on the same path. They appear as if they are standing still. The laws of attraction really do pull people together. It's so subjective that it's difficult to see until time gives us some distance away from others, to stand back and assess the changes in me, and the lack of changes in them. It's like walking up to the wrong grocery cart, it doesn't feel right. There is no fit. It's sad at first. I find myself wishing others that I once cared deeply about were on the same path, but they're not, and nothing I say or do will change that until they're inspired to change for their own reasons. Now there is distance between us, a gap with no bridge. Conversations are brief, they lack that old spark, that connection. We are different and yet they haven't changed. That is the down side. Something is lost when something is gained. It's okay, it just means they're on a different path. I experienced this dynamic at my first high school reunion, the ten year gathering. I remember walking away thinking that if I didn't see most of these people again it would be okay. Some were in the same place they were ten years earlier, still strumming the same single string on their guitars."

Listening to John, I remembered a line from the film Educating Rita, with Michael Caine who plays a college professor who helps a barely literate cockney hair stylist, played wonderfully by Julie Walters. In a single moment of awareness, when she recognizes in herself the Pygmalion transformation, she realizes the change in her perceptions and values. When, as they sit around the pub singing the old pub songs, her mother asks why she is not singing, she responds in a kind of melancholy tone, with real sadness in her voice, "There must be different songs to sing." No one in her family understands, it's like a private joke for one.

In an instant, she is gone, never to return. Things will never be the same.

John suddenly sensed he was doing all the talking. He hesitated for a moment and I said, "This is great, please continue. What else do you remember about Len?"

Thinking for a moment, he replied, "I remember the last time we spoke, he said to me very calmly, 'Why don't you THINK AND GROW RICH? Where do you think I borrowed that from?' 'Isn't that the title of a book?' I asked. 'Yes,' he said, 'I suggest you go to the bookstore and read it. Just read the first 10 pages. If you don't relate to it all, walk away. If you can relate to the points he makes in the book, resolve to invest in the purchase of the book. Fair enough?' 'Fair enough,' I replied.

"'John, I usually read a book or two a week. Do you know why I choose books? Books take an author about

20 years to write. Napoleon Hill interviewed 500 of the most successful business people in the country for over 20 years and then wrote that book. For just a few dollars, you can tap into the minds and experiences of some of the smartest people in the world. Invest a portion of your income into your own personal development.

"'Ben Franklin said, *If you take a coin from your purse and invest it in your mind, it will come flowing out of your mind and overflow your purse.* What do you suppose he meant?' Thinking for a moment, I said, 'I suppose he meant books will always give you a good return on investment.' 'Yes!' he shouted. 'The best kind of return. Intellectual capital.'"

John, recalling with a blend of pride and melancholy, continued. "As I walked away and headed for the bookstore to buy the book and journal, I smiled, thinking how fortunate I was to have found this person. Then a quote from my childhood popped into my head: *When the student is ready to learn, the teacher shows up.* He had indeed. For the first time in many years, feelings of gratitude emerged in me, and it felt wonderful. Over the next year, I began to draw strength from books, mostly biographies of great men and women who all had overcome tremendous adversity, far greater than I had. Did you know Teddy Roosevelt lost his wife and mother on the same day? Yet he bounced back even stronger. Abe Lincoln, in addition to losing the only woman he truly loved, lost almost every election he ever entered, Nine in all! Did you know that Winston Churchill was shunned by his peers, a political outcast for almost 20 years, from 1922 to 1942?

"I found strength and hope in books. Len pointed the way. He would say, 'Have you ever read about Napoleon, or General Robert E. Lee?' Before I knew it, I was back at the Battle of Gettysburg in "The Killer Angels," by Michael Shaara. Great books have changed my life. I owe that to Len. I never would have considered blending my learning with my goals. Len showed me how to become an expert in my field, by reading everything I could find on my industry and chosen profession. He once said to me, '*If you simply read 30 minutes every day in your field, you'll become an expert in your field in very short time. Remember, John, all leaders are readers.*' So simple.

"I had to come here to pay tribute to my teacher. I flew in from Columbia, South Carolina on the red-eye. I would not have missed this for the world. I owe him more than I can ever repay. You know, the crazy thing is, when I tried to pay him back, he just said, 'When the time is right, you'll have a chance to repay the debt: the student will appear. When that happens you'll know what to do.' I've tried to do just that. It doesn't make sense, 'Give it away to keep it.' Because of Len, I've done just that and my life has been blessed. You know, you're the first person I've ever told. Somehow I knew you knew. Does that make sense?"

"Perfect and complete sense," I said. "It will stay our secret. Fair enough?" We both smiled. That was Len's favorite phrase... *fair enough*.

Here is what I remember as he reeled off seven quotes that were familiar to me. I just smiled and listened. I knew them all by heart...

Len's Lessons
Journal Entries on Readers Read...

"All leaders are readers."

"Remember, you are the same today as you'll be in five years except for two things: the people you meet and the books you read. Choose both carefully." **Charlie "Tremendous" Jones**

"The books you don't read won't help." Jim Rohn

"People that don't read good books are no better off than those that don't know how to read. It's a sort of chosen illiteracy." **Mark Twain**

"Be a student, not a follower. Read two or three books on a subject, then make up your own mind."

"Invest 30 minutes a day in reading books that will make you stretch. Avoid the easy stuff. You won't grow. 30 minutes a day for six months will make you one of the most knowledgeable people in your office. After a year, in your town; two years, the county; five years, in the state; ten years, in the country; 15 years, in the world. All for just half an hour a day!"

"Insure your reading is in alignment with your goals. Read everything you can find on your goals and your profession. It's the best investment you can make."

"Take a coin from your purse and invest it in your mind. It will coming pouring out of your mind and overflow your purse." **Ben Franklin**

Chapter 3

"Attitude Alters Altitude"

Len's oldest son had an opportunity to speak at his father's funeral. He had grown up to be a fine young man—successful, well spoken, and articulate. He began, "I learned a great many things from my father. I learned how to love from my father. Evidently, my Dad had always had a compassionate heart. My Grandfather told me about a time when Dad was five years old. In the old neighborhood, on the poor side of town, back in the forties, an elderly couple lived next door. They had been married for over fifty years when the wife was lost to cancer. The day after the funeral, the old widower was sitting on the porch swing he and his wife used to sit in. My dad, while having dinner with the family, saw him sitting there alone. He got up half way through the meal without saying a word and went out the door. This was not normal behavior for Dad—dinner was his favorite meal and he loved to eat. Grandma got up and looked out the window to see what he was up to. She saw him climb up onto the old man's lap. About 20 minutes later, Dad gave him a hug and came back into the house, still not saying a word, and resumed eating his cold dinner. Finally, Grandma couldn't stand it anymore and asked him what they had talked about. Dad thought for a minute and said, 'Oh, we didn't talk. I just helped him cry.'"

As I looked around the church, there wasn't a dry eye in the house.

"That was the first and only time I ever heard about Dad talking about the people he helped. He never talked about the work he did for others, not to me, not to my brother, or to my mom. When we asked, he'd say, 'Oh, I'll tell you someday.' He was a very private man. Yet the overwhelming turnout today clearly shows that he helped a lot of people. You can't know how much it means to our family to have you all here to celebrate my Dad's life. Thank you for coming and helping *me* cry."

I couldn't help but feel a little jealous knowing his son would get to read his father's journals. He was unique. Imagine—hundreds of journals in Len's own hand. I smiled when I considered all the thoughts, lessons, insights, and wisdom.

I remember one particular day, I was frustrated by my apparent snail's pace of growth, specifically regarding optimism and seeing things the way Len seemed to. "Have you ever considered your impact on others, Steve?" Len asked softly. "No, I haven't," I replied meekly. "That's obvious!" he said to me sternly. "Optimism is a learned behavior and attitude. It has a number of components. The way I see it, it's kind of like a set of binoculars. When good things happen to me, I look at them through the magnified end. The good in my life becomes larger and more enjoyable. When the bad things happen I take responsibility for them but look at them through the minimizing end, thereby capturing the learning without dwelling on them or making them bigger than they need to be. Which way do you turn your binoculars when positive things happen? I would hazard a guess you developed the habit of seeing them the opposite of what I just described. Here are some things to remember:

1. Optimism requires constant fanning.

2. Optimists capture their WINS in writing!

3. Optimists believe GOOD EVENTS stem from permanent conditions and are the direct results of their efforts and attitudes.

4. Optimists believe BAD EVENTS stem from temporary conditions and external causes. They find temporary and specific causes for misfortune, yet take full responsibility for it. (That is the Art of Hope!)

5. Optimists like themselves and have a healthy sense of self: Self-Respect.

6. Optimists catch themselves and others doing things right: Praise pays.

7. Optimists believe they CAN CHANGE and rewrite any aspect of their life's script.

After the funeral, I spoke with his son Daniel. What would he miss the most? He thought for a minute and said, "Hearing him say, 'son, I'm proud of you. I'm glad you're my son.' Growing up, I heard him say that almost every day.

"I also liked his responses to the question, 'How are you doing today?' He always had an unusual or funny response," Daniel said, grinning. "Do you remember?"

"Yes," I said, reeling off the following:

- "Fabulous"
- "Sensational"
- "Incredible"
- "Stupendous"
- "A notch above Awesome"
- "I'm on this side of the grass"
- "If I was doing any better, I'd be twins"

"At night he used to ask us two questions: 'What was the most fun you had today?' After I'd go on about the highlight of my day, I would feel safe, secure, and good inside. Then he'd ask me, 'What are you looking forward to tomorrow?' He just listened, you know? I felt like he really cared and understood. I remember hearing him say, 'people need three things, son:

1. Appreciation

2. Respect

3. Understanding.

"'Are you giving that to others?' A.R.U. Dad liked acronyms. It was how he remembered things that were important to him."

"You loved him a lot," I said.

"Yes, I'm really gonna miss him," Daniel said softly.

"Me too. I'm going to miss his SMILE too, that toothy grin for no apparent reason. He used to say, '*smile and the feelings will follow. If you smile long enough, you'll come up with a good reason to.*' Did he ever have you make a 'Gratitude list?' I asked Daniel."

"All the time," Daniel replied with a smile. "That used to really annoy me, give me five things you're grateful for on paper?!? Now I understand. It's a simple way to shift my focus from the wrong things to the right ones."

"He was something, wasn't he. Different," I mused.

"I've never known anyone else quite like him," Daniel said softly, a hint of sadness in his voice. "He was really a student. He was constantly taking notes. I remember asking him why one day. He said, 'Every person I meet is my superior in some way.' I later came across that quote in an essay by Ralph Waldo Emerson."

"Thanks for spending time with me, Daniel. You're a lot like your Dad. Your children are lucky."

Len's Lessons
Journal Entries on *Attitude Alters Altitude*

"Every man I meet is my superior in some way..."
Ralph Waldo Emerson

"Consider this: How can I develop an attitude of gratitude in all things? Answer? List five things you are grateful for today on paper!"

"Smile and feelings will follow. If you smile long enough, you'll come up with a reason."

"Finding temporary and specific causes for misfortune is the 'Art of Hope.' Finding permanent and universal causes of misfortune is the 'Practice of Despair.' Which one do you practice?" **M. Seligman**

"The last of Human Freedoms is to choose one's attitude in any given set of circumstances."
Victor Frankl

Chapter 4

"Journaling the Journey"

Sitting in the church, my mind wandered back to a memory of Len. We were in the coffee shop where we spent so many mornings. He said to me, "The palest ink is better than the strongest memory." He must have said that a hundred times. He always had a pen and paper with him. He took notes in books, on 3 x 5 cards, on napkins, and it all eventually ended up in his journal. *"If it's worth remembering, it's worth writing down."*

"Why do you invest so much time in journaling?" I asked.

"Well, some people try to get through the day. I aspire to get FROM it. There is a difference." He went on to say, "Journals provide opportunities for reflection, serious thought, objectivity and real learning of oneself. It is one of the finest disciplines and personal development tools available and yet not one man in 100 will invest the time, the discipline, the effort to capture his thoughts on paper. I have found when I have a challenge, it allows me to create a solution; when I have a fear, it shows me how futile

and small that fear really is. It's a trusted friend, the kind that never lets me down, always has time for me and my concerns. All great people of the past from Abraham Lincoln and Winston Churchill, to Theodore Roosevelt, to Mahatma Gandhi, to John F. Kennedy, all kept a diary, a journal. It is the finest way to pass on your philosophy and beliefs to your children and grandchildren. A shade tree that everyone will be able to sit under. What a tremendous legacy to leave your heirs, if you really think about it, a little piece of immortality. Journals and books last forever. The more time passes, the more valuable they become. Nothing else is quite like a journal."

"You feel pretty passionate about your journals, don't you?" I observed.

Len smiled. "Yes, you noticed. Sometimes I get carried away. The discipline of journaling has had a profound and positive effect on not just my life but on the lives of my children. They both keep a journal. I'm proud of them.

"I started in my mid-twenties while my wife and I were on a trip to Mexico. My mother had given me a 'Travel Journal' to capture the memories. I filled that book up with detail after detail of the most enjoyable trip we had been on together. I wrote a page a day for ten days. It wasn't until later, when a friend asked me about my trip and where he should eat when he and his wife were down there, that I even pulled it out to reread it. It was at that moment it struck me—I had used the journal to plan, record, and capture the details of the trip. It had become this amazing jewel box, this magical moment in time for all eternity. Then the real truth came flying through, a blinding flash of the obvious. Why had the trip been so successful? Why had it been so memorable? Why did things go so well? It was the thought and energy that we had put into it because of the journal. What if I put that same energy into the other 50 weeks of the year? What if I flip-flopped the process? What if I invested the same energy, time and effort into planning and recording my life? Would I achieve the same kinds of results?

That is precisely what I did. The life well designed. I gave up all accountability for future vacations over the next ten years to my wife (she was far more qualified anyway), and began designing the next decade the same way I had designed the previous vacations."

"What happened?" I asked with anticipation.

"Well, precisely the same kind of powerful result. I began asking myself:

What do I want to see?

What do I want to do?

What will I need to learn?

From that moment on, my life exploded into change."

"That's amazing. Just by writing it down?" I inquired.

"Yes," Len replied, "anyone can do it. You already have the experience and skill required to complete the job, it's simply a matter of shifting attitudes and thought processes from vacations to your professional life. It's just that simple. Amazing, isn't it? The best things in life are both simple and free. I like to think of it as Aladdin's Magic Lamp. The difference is, you are granted more than three wishes. However, I've found it's best to ask for one wish at a time."

"Where do I start?" I asked enthusiastically.

"Good question," Len said, "let me answer by telling you a true story. I was in Jail one day... as a visitor. A friend of mine, his name is Matt, runs the jail program for inmates that want to change their lives for good. He asked me to sit in on his class and address the group at the end of the session. While I sat there, I heard some fascinating things coming from these inmates. Most of them were anxious to change and to get out of jail. They were very teachable. There was one man, however, who told the group in very clear terms that he had no intention of leaving. You see, he had become institutionalized. You could hear it in his self-talk. All I heard from him that morning was blaming, complaining and explaining. From an objective and learning point of view it was fascinating, yet it broke my heart. I knew he would spend the rest of his life going <u>in</u> and out of jail or prison. He had become more comfortable in jail than out. As I took notes, he interrupted one of his fellow inmates with a mildly sarcastic comment directed toward me. You see, my journal has a very nice leather cover with a rather ornate design. He said, loud enough for everyone to hear, 'If I had a journal like that, I'd write a lot more.'

"I thought for a moment, and considered ignoring the remark. However, it was a teachable moment, so I said in a very calm and understated way, "I started taking notes years ago… on a napkin." The room fell quiet. Almost everyone in the room understood. Message delivered, message received. My friend Matt smiled. Afterward, he commented to me, 'You know he may never leave. Do you know why they call these guys Cons? Because they are so good at 'Conning' themselves first. I was glad you spoke up. It meant something to the other guys. Thanks for coming.'"

Len's stories always had a point. As I pondered the lesson, I said, "So you're saying I should start right where I am?" He just smiled and handed me a napkin. "That's your get-out-of-jail-free card. Be certain you capture the good stuff life offers, pay attention, especially to your own self-talk first, other's second. Listen to the self-talk of successful people. What do they say when they lose? If you listen closely, you'll hear 'I'll bounce back' or 'I learned a great deal from that experience.' Be mindful, the learning is all around."

So, the first thing I did was buy a journal. That really wasn't hard, I had written things down for as long as I could remember. Writing came easily to me, though it had been a long time since I had done any real writing. Then, with Len's guidance and advice, I began designing the life I now live, first in my imagination, then on paper. I became my own travel agent. I booked the plans and designed the itinerary of my life. I had no idea the results would happen so quickly. After I processed the grief that struck me when I realized I had wasted a great deal of time, I began to pour my energies into the 50 weeks a year that were important to me and my new life began moving toward me at a very rapid pace.

Len once pulled out his journal and showed me his incredible book. It had a nice leather cover on the outside and was filled with quotes, ideas, articles, pictures, goals, sketches, a patchwork, a veritable quilt of information in different color ink. I remember thinking I would love to read it. As if he was able to see that thought, he said, "You won't ever get to read my journal. I don't share its contents with anyone, it's very personal. The only people who will get to read it will be my two boys after I'm dead. If they decide to share with anyone after I'm gone, that's their decision. You see, a journal is a very private thing.

It's meant for myself alone. Occasionally I will share an entry or two with someone if I feel it will help them at that moment. However, not to worry, you will fill up plenty of journals from today forward."

Len's Lessons
Journal Entries on *Journaling the Journey*

"The palest ink is better than the strongest memory."

"Some people try to get THROUGH the day, I aspire to get FROM it!"

"If it is worth remembering, it's worth writing down."

"All great figures of history kept a journal. Greatness is measured by our contribution to others."

"If reading is water, when you pour water into your glass, most people stop when they get to the top. However, if you keep pouring, the water will spill onto the table and, hopefully, the floor. What is on the table is your writing. You have no choice once you spill. Keep pouring."

Chapter 5
"Solitude, Silence and Serenity"

Robert, his youngest son, stepped up to the podium and began talking about his Dad. "He was a spiritual man, but at times he could cuss like a sailor on liberty. I guess that's what made him real. He was never phony. If he was mad, you knew it. If he was sad, he cried. If he was hungry, he was a bear (he used to walk around grumbling something about low blood sugar). He talked about his Father, and I knew he didn't mean his Dad. It was the source of his inner strength, a sort of higher power he would tap into from time to time. He had a strange habit of praying for people he didn't like. He used to say, 'Darkness cannot exist in the light.' About once a month, he would make a list of people that annoyed him, that he had negative feelings toward, then I would hear him praying for those people. Funny thing was, I saw him heal a lot of pain, and I used to be amazed at his ability to get a strained relationship back on track with this method. It wasn't a trick, or a manipulation: he meant it. He said some of his old habits were hard wired and took time to overcome. But you know something? He was always working on it. I admired him for that. I was nine-teen when I finally understood what he meant when he said, 'The quality of my life is proportionate to the quality of my relationships.'

"He used to get up early, five a.m., almost every day. He used to call it his 'solitude time.' I used to think he was crazy. Not anymore. He used to say, 'Hey, I can always take a nap this afternoon.' And he did. He used to tell us about famous nappers of the 20th century: Winston Churchill, John F. Kennedy, Tom Edison, Bill Gates. His affinity to learn about greatness, the qualities that the great figures of history possessed, was definitely a pas-sionate pursuit. He was very curious about what drove and inspired men and women who had achieved amaz-ing things in their lives. He would say that they had a *Magnificent Obsession*. Then he would smile.

"During his Solitude Time, he would read, write in his journal, pray, and sometimes just sit there. He used to say, 'Be still and know that I am God.' When I asked him what that meant, he'd say that it was the Bible boiled down to its essence. Lowly listening. Most of my best ideas come to me in that solitude time, but it's hard work. Listening is not easy at first. It takes practice. Like a mus-cle, it becomes stronger with use.

"Once a year, he would go on a personal retreat. It was his solitude time. I remember hearing him say once, 'There is a big difference between feeling lonely and being alone.' He would pack up a box full of food, his journals from the last year, a good book and say 'I'll see you in a few days.' He especially liked the ocean. Something about the sound of the waves crashing against the shore, it connected him, somehow, to nature. Like Henry David Thoreau, he also liked investing time in the woods. Solitude. There was no television, no friends, no work, just some time alone for planning, but mostly for reflection. He would call us, however, about every other day. I was to find out years later, about age 23, what he would do. He consistently asked himself the following questions:

1. What was the most fun I had this past year?

2. What did I learn this past year?

3. What did I change for good this past year?

4. What mistakes had the most positive impact on me this past year?

5. What bad habits did I pick up this past year?

6. What books had the biggest impact on me this past year?

Then he would ask himself:

1. What important projects would I like to complete

this next year?

2. What am I looking forward to in my personal life this next year?

3. What skills would I like to sharpen this next year?

4. What books will help me the most this next year?

5. How can I increase my service to others this next year?

6. How much would I like to earn this next year?

"He gave me a bookmark once that Mom had given him that had a special poem inscribed upon it. I would like to read it. It's called *You Must Not Quit!*

YOU MUST NOT QUIT!

When things go wrong as they sometimes will,
When the road you're trudging seems all uphill,
When the funds are low, and the debts are high,
When you want to smile but you have to sigh,
When care is pressing you down a bit,
Rest if you must, but don't you quit.

Life is strange with its twists and turns,
As every one of us sometimes learns,
And many a failure was turned about,

When he might have won had he stuck it out.
Don't give up, though the pace seems slow,
You may succeed with another blow.

Success is failure turned inside out,
The silver tint of clouds of doubt,
And you never can tell how close you are,
It may be near when it seems so far.
So stick in the fight when you are hardest hit,
It's when things seem worst,
That YOU MUST NOT QUIT!"

"'The door of the soul opens inward,' said Len. You must be still to know God. That's why we don't always enjoy God's will. We assume that the door opens outward. We press and push against it as hard as we can, seemingly oblivious to the fact that we are really closing it all the more firmly against our own good. It is simply trying to overcome by human effort, and leaving God out. To work in this way is really to use *will* power and not *way* power. In Buddhism, 'The Way' is the less traveled path, the simpler path, the easier path.

"Human nature is very prone to push blindly when frustrated or frightened. Indeed, this is precisely why the doors on public buildings and theatres are obliged by law to open outward, by pushing. It is the natural direction of panic, fear. Prayer, however, is essentially the refusal to be rushed by panic, or by the existing current of things. In prayer, you must draw back from the outer picture, cease to press against events, and realize the presence of God. The door of the soul opens inward, go to the closet and shut the door and be still. It takes practice and persistence. Don't you quit, it's worth the effort."

Len's Lessons
Solitude, Silence and Serenity

"Be still and know that I am God."

"Make an appointment with yourself every day... and keep your word to yourself."

"Make the time for 'Lowly-Listening.' It's hard work, but worth the effort."

"There is a big difference between loneliness and being alone. It's possible to be lonely in a crowded room."

"Reflection is a powerful discipline. The formula is as follows: end of the day, reflect for 15 minutes; end of the week, reflect for 30 minutes; end of the month, for an hour; end of the quarter, for two hours; end of the year, reflect for a day."

Chapter 6

"Labor of Love"

The next speaker was very tall and displayed a great deal of quiet confidence as he stepped up to the podium. "The day I met Len changed my life forever." Frank spoke with a powerful voice and a commanding presence. He was a lean, handsome man, impeccably dressed. "I was a 32 year old Heating and Air-Conditioning Technician. I was a likeable enough fellow and if you were to ask my boss, he would have said I was a pretty good hand with a wrench, but there was something missing from my life."

As I sat and listened to this fellow, I thought to myself, *this guy was never a blue-collar worker. He is so eloquent, articulate and composed.* "I met Len one hot summer day in August. I had already done at least six calls that day. It must have been at least 5:30 in the afternoon when I pulled up to Len's building. He was the owner. We had never done work on his building before. The repair was a simple one, and I was done in a few minutes. While I was writing up the work order, Len started asking me some questions. He was genuinely interested in his building's environmental system and what had gone wrong so that we might avoid the same problem in the future. It was refreshing to deal with someone like him. Once we were done with business, he said, 'As good as you are at your job, I sense you are not happy in your work. There is an underlying sadness in you. Do you want to talk about it?' How did he know? Was it that obvious?

"'I've worked with my hands for ten years,' I answered. 'I started when I was just 16 years old. Recently, I've been saying to myself, *I don't want to do this anymore, but I can't just quit. I have a mortgage, a wife, a baby boy, and I don't want to walk away from ten years of experience in the industry.'*

"'You seem like a bright young man that just needs some direction,' Len responded. 'If I were to introduce you to someone who could help you clarify some things, would you pay him a visit?'

"'Yes, thank you, I would,' I replied.

"The next day, I went into the company owner's office and asked to speak with him. Karl seemed to be a very spiritual man, approachable, kind, honest, and caring. I told him how frustrated I was, not with the industry, but with my role in it. What would he do if he were in my shoes? Smiling ruefully, he said, 'I am honored that you asked me. I can only tell you what I would do and have done that has worked for me. I will help you on two simple conditions: One, that you never tell anyone that I helped you. Two, at some point in the future, you help someone else just for the sake of service, not with any expectation of receiving any reward or recognition. Fair enough?' he said with a strange smile.

"'Fair enough,' I said hesitantly."

Frank paused for a moment in his story. In that brief moment, I reflected back. Hmmm, Karl... that was Len's mentor, wasn't it? Yes, he was Len's mentor, his first real teacher and coach. I remember Len talking about this guy with great reverence.

Frank continued his story. "'When I was forty,' Karl said, 'I decided to build a larger house for my growing family. I sat down with the contractor and the architect and we drew up the plans. We started with a completed project and began to work backwards. If I were you, that's what I would do. You must have a plan.' That is what Karl said to me. I grabbed a pen and a notepad, and I captured the questions he shared with me. He continued with his barrage as my pen captured every word.

"'Perhaps the best way I can help you is to ask you some questions that will assist you in clarifying your direction and identifying your strengths and areas where you have an unidentified passion. First you must answer some very fundamental questions:

- What do you love to do?

- What comes easily for you that is hard for others?

- What would you do for no money. Simply stated, If all the jobs paid a dollar, which one would you want?

- If you had only six months to live, how would you spend your time?

"My head was spinning," said Frank. "I had never given any real thought to these kinds of questions.

"'Once you answer these questions on paper, come back and see me. Fair enough?' asked Karl.

"'Fair enough,' I replied. It was something in the way he said *What do you love to do*. He emphasized the word love with such passion, enthusiasm and certainty. I knew he was doing what he loved. You could see it in his eyes. As I was leaving, he said to me, 'Frank, if you love what you do and do what you love, you will never work - another day in your life. Remember this: if you do what you love, the money will follow!' Advice coming from someone as successful as Karl really meant something to me.

"Over the course of the next six weeks, I answered

dozens of questions and for the first time in my life, got in touch with my inner self. Karl suggested that I 'soar with my strengths' and advised me to 'Get bigger than my job by studying the business of business.' Then one day, he shocked me by saying, 'I would like to introduce you to an old friend of mine. He used to work for me five years ago. He was my top salesman. His name is Jim. He left to start his own company and he needs a good salesman. Are you interested in having lunch with him?' I couldn't believe my ears! Here was Karl, the owner of my company introducing me to his direct competitor for a job as a salesman. Didn't he know if I accepted a job with Jim, I would probably take business away from him? I was confused. Then, as though he could read my mind, he said, 'You probably think it's strange I would introduce you to my competitor. You see, Frank, there is always room in any large city for another good contractor. Jim is a fine man. You would learn a lot from him. I don't have a position for you right now, and you are ready to make the transition. He needs someone with your potential. But I want you to remember our bargain. Fair enough?'

"'Yes,' I said with a smile, 'Fair enough.'

"I spent the next five years in Jim's employ, five of the most exciting and rewarding years of my life. I learned later that Karl had cancer at the time that he first helped me. That, I thought naïvely, was why he helped me transition out of his company. But my new boss told me that he would have done the same thing even if he were healthy. 'You see, Frank, when someone has the desire to get bigger than their job, and then goes to work right where they are, a BIG person will always help them. Karl was a BIG person. He understood the *Laws of Compensation*. He used to call it the unfailing boomerang. He lived in the long term. Relationships and people are what were important to him. Did you know he was worth over 500 million dollars? He owned several businesses and had helped hundreds—no, thousands—of people in his lifetime. The curious part is that he never really cared about the money. Oh, I suppose early in his career he might have, but people were always his first priority. He taught Len much of what he knows, and he did the same for me. Do you know the play *Pygmalion* by George Bernard Shaw?'

"'No,' I said, with a little bit of embarrassment.

"'It was later adapted into the musical comedy *My Fair Lady*.'

"'Yes,' I said, 'I've seen that on TV. Wasn't that about a flower girl who was turned into a lady by a teacher and a colonel?'

"'Yes, that's the one. Karl was Colonel Pickering. He always saw me and treated me like the person I have become, even when I couldn't see it. He was a great man. He taught me a great deal before he pushed me out of the nest. I'll never forget what he said before I left his employment and started this company. *Frank, find a need and fill it, first or better. And Frank, remember, you can have anything in life you want, if you only assist enough other people in getting what they want first. You are part of a great fraternity. It's an awesome trust carrying the torch of silence and responsibility. Once you grab hold of it, you can never let go. In exchange for that you will receive opportunity, gifts, skills, influence, personal greatness and joy that you could never have imagined previously. Welcome to the club.'"*

Len's Lessons
Labor of Love

"Do what you love and the money will follow."

"If you love what you do, you'll never work another day in your life."

"My work is play, twelve hours a day."

"If you work on your gifts, they will make room for you."

"Soar with your strengths and never look back."

"Find out what you're good at. What comes easy to you? Does anyone else make a living doing it? If yes, go ask them what they would do differently if they were starting over now. Then go to work right where you are, getting bigger than your job, until you can do it full time."

"80% of Success in Business is just showing up. Find a need and fill it first or better."

"Did you know that you can have anything you want if you only assist enough other people to get what they want first?"

Chapter 7
"Helping... Heart of Happiness"

As I sat listening to one speaker after another, I reflected on my own experiences with Len. I remember the day I finally "got it," the turning point of my life. Len whispered to me one day, an expression on his face such as I'd never seen before. It was a look full of conviction and sincerity, the kind someone gives you when they are the bearer of bad news, when a friend has died, when there is a tragedy to relate—you know, that kind of look. Len said, "Do you want the secret to life?"

"Yes," I replied, "very much."

"Helping others... it's the Heart of Happiness," Len said softly. "<u>Service to Others</u>."

You could have heard a pin drop. I was expecting something profound. Seeing that I wasn't getting it, he continued. "Let me explain with a story. About ten years ago, I was having breakfast in Fort Worth on a warm

Texas morning with a friend. As we left the restaurant, we passed a mother in crisis. She had two boys, about four and seven, and the younger one had spilled his pancake syrup all over his lap. It wasn't the temperature of the spilt syrup that was doing the most damage, it was the embarrassment of the public accident. He was crying and inconsolable. Mom was struggling with the mess on his Sunday best, no time to deal with his little feelings. As I passed, I leaned down and gently whispered loud enough for Mom and brother to hear, 'I wish I had a dollar for every time I spilled something at the table. Heck, at 42 years old, I still do that sometimes. It's gonna be okay.' Judging by the face of the little guy, it really was going to be okay. He was allowed to save face."

"Len, you didn't even know these people. Why was it so important?" I asked naïvely.

"Saving face in some countries is cause for suicide. Well, having spilled many things as a kid, and growing up with an overwhelming sense of feeling *less than*, I believe it's about the restoration of our human dignity. Our mistakes are acknowledged as just that... mistakes. That little boy would not have done that on purpose. Eleanor Roosevelt once said, 'No one can make you feel inferior without your consent.' She forgot to add 'And that includes my consent.' That little kid in the diner had not given himself permission to forgive himself. He didn't understand we all make mistakes, spill things, drop things, break things, but not with *intention*. They are just things. He was being human. Human beings do dumb stuff, silly stuff, and careless stuff. I just gave him permission to be human. The difference is, once you understand that, you transition to a Human *Becoming*. There is a difference. If I am *becoming*, I am in a sort of state of grace. It took me a long time to learn that."

Len continued, "My motive for helping that little guy had a little to do with enlightened self-interest. *I knew how I would feel afterward!* I walked out into that Texas morning feeling great, knowing I had done my good deed for the day. What price did I pay for this fabulous feeling? It cost me about twenty seconds of my time, a little empathy and a little thought. In exchange, the world was a little easier for that four-year-old in Fort Worth. Although "Saving Face" is not usually on the menu, you can order it any time. Best of all, it always tastes great. You see, I can change how I feel at any moment simply by helping someone else! If I am full of anger, self-pity, resentment, jealousy, FEAR, I can change that. If I recognize my negative state of mind and claim it, name it, it begins to loosen its hold on me. Then, if I begin to look for the kid with the syrup in his lap and offer up some assistance, it changes me. I feel different. The negativity falls off me like a loose rope around Houdini's waist.

"This business of helping others, it just takes keen observation, a willingness to risk, a little thoughtfulness, and practice. You can start at home. Begin with your significant other. How can you ease her burden? You can try it with your children or grandchildren. What do they need? There are lots of ways to help people. One of the best ways I have found is to just listen. One of the finest gifts you can give someone is the gift of your attention. Listening is a skill and discipline that takes time to develop. Active listening is to listening what geometry is to algebra. It's math but at a different level of awareness. Listening is the vehicle for understanding. Understanding is how trust and solid long-term relationships are built. Men, in particular, sadly lack this vital interpersonal skill. We have been conditioned 'Not to Listen.' Most of us are simply waiting to talk.

"Understanding requires several things. I call it giving others their DUE. DUE is Desire, *Understanding* and *Empathy:*

1. *Desire* to Understand. You must *want* to.

2. *Understanding* the value of understanding in the human condition.

3. *Empathy*, the ability to stand in someone else's shoes and comprehend how they feel. It's not sympathy, but empathy, that builds trust and long-term relationships.

"Another requirement is your time. Yet another is your skills and gifts. What are you good at? You can begin right where you are.

"St. Francis had it right when he wrote, 'seek to understand, then to be understood.' One person that understood that, and lived it, was Will Rogers. He was a humorist, cowboy, philosopher, philanthropist, statesman, writer, speaker, movie star, father and husband. He said, *'I never met a man I didn't like.'* There is a statue of him in Washington, D.C. that has those words carved in it for all eternity, and they summarize the philosophy and attitude that were responsible for endearing him to millions of Americans. Will Rogers truly made a difference in many people's lives. Franklin Roosevelt wrote in a letter to Will's friend, Walter Harrison:

"'We remember Will Rogers with gratitude and affection because he knew how to revive the spirit of laughter in hearts that had known too much of the distractions and anxieties of a busy world. His mission in life was to cheer, to comfort, and to console.

"'There was something infectious about his humor. His appeal went straight to the heart of the nation. Above all things, in a time grown too solemn and somber, he brought his countrymen back to a sense of proportion.

"'Will Rogers knew out of the fullness of a blithe

heart that few things in life are to be taken seriously and that our troubles multiply if we take them
tragically. And so he showed us all how to laugh.
From him, we can learn anew the homely lesson
that the way to make progress is to build on what
we have, to believe that today is better than yesterday and that tomorrow will be better than
either.'"

What does Will Rogers have to do with Len, you might
ask? The two had much in common. I discovered Will
through Len. He gave me Will's biography, and it was
clear the two were related in spirit. You see, the philanthropist in Will would do anything for the downtrodden,
the underdog, the victims. Len was like that. He had a gift
for being able to see pain and readiness in the same person in just a few minutes. However, he was always qual-
ifying your commitment to yourself by asking questions
like, "If I give you this book from my library, will you read
it? How soon?" In a way, he was a preacher of the Gospel
of Accountability. He was not of the school of self-reliance
that Emerson preached 135 years ago, but he did preach
and live the accountability creed nonetheless.

He would help you if you were willing to help yourself.
He would say to me, "If you take one step, I'll take two. If
I make the time, you must honor your commitment to
yourself." He was big on Integrity. Keeping your word to
yourself. He would say, "If you don't have self-respect,

how can you respect others? If you don't like yourself, how can you like others? You can't give away something you don't have. Heck, even on an airplane, the stewardess, when explaining how the oxygen mask will pop down in the event of an emergency, warns parents to put their own masks on first, then assist the child." What a great analogy, I thought to myself. He had a way of putting things simply.

Len's Lessons
Journal entries: *Helping... the Heart of Happiness*

"Helping others is the Heart of Happiness. Service to others is the secret to a joyful life."

"It really is true that you can have everything you want in life, IF you help enough other people get what they want."

"If I give you this book from my library, will you read it?"

"No one can make you feel inferior without your consent." **Eleanor Roosevelt**

"I have no right to say or do anything that diminishes a man in his own eyes. What matters is not what I think of him, but what he thinks of himself. Hurting a man in his dignity is a crime." **Antoine de Saint-Exupery**

"I never met a man I didn't like." **Will Rogers**

"To make progress is to build on what we have, to believe that today is better than yesterday, and tomorrow will be better than either!"

"We can't keep something until we give it away. Sharing what we know with others is the pathway to peace and enlightenment."

Chapter 8

"Time Takes Time"

Time takes time. I was thinking about that when the next speaker said to the gathering in the church, "What do you want written on your tombstone?" It was exactly what I needed to hear to shake up my thinking.

Her name was Margaret. She had flown in from Guam, of all places, to speak at Len's funeral. She was a nurse, a very famous nurse. She proceeded to tell her story.

"One day, Len said to me, 'Let's go get some coffee at that Starbucks and talk.' That little phrase was the beginning of a life change. 'Time takes time. Start slow,' he said. 'You didn't get this way overnight. It will take some time to change for good. Take it easy. Remember: measurable progress in reasonable time.'

"He continued, 'Let me see your list of goals. Maybe that is the best way I can help you right now.'

"'I don't have them,' I said, embarrassed.

"'Are they in your car?'

"'No.'

"'Oh, maybe they're at your house. We can swing by there.'

"'No, I don't have them anywhere. I don't have any goals written down, never have,' I said meekly.

"'OH... I see,' he said softly. 'Well, that's where we'll start. Take this pen and paper and let's get started. Imagine you are in a very large church. As you walk in you suddenly get a strange feeling, like a cold chill or a déjà vu. You look around and notice something odd: you know almost everyone there. You walk to the front of the church to pay your respects to the deceased, you look down into the casket and, lo and behold, it's you lying there! You comment to the person next to you how odd that is, and you realize they can't hear you. Feeling like you're in a Twilight Zone episode, you sit down in back to listen to four speakers: your spouse of many years, your best friend, your business partner or boss and a good friend that worked with you in your community. What will they say about you? I'll let you think about that for the next thirty minutes. Write down whatever comes to mind. Fair enough?'

"'Yes, I understand,' I replied. As Len got up to get some more coffee and chat with the barista, I began my strange exercise.

"When I was done, Len said, 'What did you learn?'

"'I'm not sure I did this right. What was I supposed to write? I could only think of all the negative stuff, which I knew was not right. No one says anything negative at a funeral about someone they cared about. What I ended up writing was what I would WANT them to say about me. So how did I do?'

"'You did just fine. There is no right way to do this, it's designed to help you appreciate how little time you have and to identify the gap between where you are and where you would like to be before you die. You had several significant distinctions. Great job! Now let's run the next leg of the race. I want you to make out a dream list, a lifetime goal list. What do you want to:

1. Have?

2. Do?

3. See?

4. Become?

5. Share?

"'Invest another thirty minutes or so and write down as many things as you can think of, try for ten in each category. When you are done, we will go over the fifty things you have written down, fair enough?' he asked warmly.

"'Fair enough!'

"This particular exercise was really hard at first. I started slowly. It was hard to think in these terms. I had too many lids on my container. However, after about fifteen minutes, it really lit my fire. By the time I was done, the pen was flying across the paper and I didn't want to stop. I felt like a little kid at Christmas.

"Len could see I was visibly excited. He smiled. 'Congratulations,' he said enthusiastically. 'You have just come up with fifty things to live for. This list will add fifteen or twenty years to your life. You now have many things to look forward to! One word of caution: make sure you review your list every year and cross off the goals you have accomplished. This will make you feel great. More importantly, when you cross one off, add at least one more to the list—no matter how outlandish it sounds.' He opened up his journal and read me a few of his:

DO:

- Golf at St. Andrews in Scotland with Dean.

- Dive the Great Barrier Reef in Australia.

- Walk the Great Wall of China with my family.

- Ride down the Nile at Sunset with my Boys.

- Explore Machu Picchu in Peru.

SHARE:

- Write 3 bestselling children's books to help kids feel better about themselves and donate the proceeds to a good literacy fund.

- Help build a community center for kids that teaches reading and writing skills, self-reliance, and life skills.

"As Len shared some of his lifetime goals, it was apparent that his thinking was much bigger than mine. He was truly a possibility thinker. He had big dreams. I also noticed he had checked off about half of his goals! Wow! I was really on to something here. This was amazing. Len said to me, 'When you commit your dreams to paper, something magical happens. It's the power of the Quantified Objective. When you write it down, you begin to move toward the goal… and it begins to move toward you. Asking begins the receiving process. We usually get whatever we ask for. Most of us have not learned to ask intelligently or without limits. Congratulations, you are in the elite 5% of the population that has a lifetime goal list. You're on your way!

"'Now, I want you to remember a few things that might help. In fact, why don't you write them down. Remember: Time takes time. Do first things first. Do one thing at a time. Finish what you start. Make the time to plan every single day, even on the weekends. We only have so much time.'

"My pen was writing like crazy. 'Are you a morning person or an evening person?' Len inquired.

"'Morning,' I replied firmly. 'Definitely Mornings.'

"'Okay,' Len said softly, 'Tomorrow morning, try this next little discipline and then do it for the next thirty days without fail. After you review your goals, ask yourself, *what can I do today to move me toward my number one goal?* As you plan your workday, weave an activity into your day that will move you one step closer to your goal.

"'This next bit of advice is vital: One goal at a time! I put mine onto a 3 x 5 card and it sits on my dash next to the speedometer. That way I see it every day, five or six times a day. When I am stuck in traffic, I read it aloud with enthusiasm. I am amazed at the ideas that bubble to the surface when I am driving. Give it a try, what have you got to lose? I have been doing this now for over 30 years… one goal at a time.

"'Finally, throughout the day, ask yourself, what is the best use of my time right now? I believe you will have a lot of fun with these ideas. They work!'

"I floated out of the Starbucks that day," Margaret said proudly. "I was filled with the possibilities of life and a new found enthusiasm and faith. From that day to this, I have never stopped the process. I have been to fifteen countries, accomplished all of my professional goals, I am living the life imagined. I never dreamed that a one hour meeting in a coffee shop with a great teacher could so profoundly alter my life in such a meaningful and lasting way. I will always be grateful for what Len did for me that day. Judging by the turnout, I wasn't the only person he helped. I think I need to sit down again and rewrite my funeral exercise. This is amazing. I sure am going to miss him."

As she stepped down from the podium I made a few notes in my journal:

Len's Lessons
Journal entries — *Time Takes Time*

"Time takes time."

"Do first things first."

"Do one thing at a time."

"Finish what you start."

"Make the time to plan every day. If you fail to plan, you are planning to fail. It only takes fifteen minutes a day. Plan your work (and your play) and work your plan. Just do it."

"What is the best use of my time right now?"

"Is what I am doing right now moving me toward my objectives? Is it helping others?"

Chapter 9

"Releasing Resilience"

"There have never been two winters in a row in 6,000 years of recorded history. Winters come and winters go. Learn to carry your weather inside you. If you can hang on, things have a way of working out. As bad as things might look at any given time, they always have a way of looking better in the morning." As Len's wife stepped up to the podium, I was thinking about a dark and scary time in my life that Len had helped me through.

She was a beautiful lady, tall, athletic and very regal. I had only met her once before, many years ago. She was a very private person. She smiled and said, "I want to thank you all for coming to this celebration of life. This turnout is overwhelming. Len would have loved this. What a pity we didn't do this while he was alive. His death was so sudden and such a shock. As sad as we all are at his death, and as bad as we all feel right now, he would have wanted this story to be told, it was one his favorites...

"A man was involved in a very serious accident one cold winter evening. Although he was seriously injured, it was a busy night in the emergency room. Consequently, he was forced to wait. Feeling sorry for himself, and in some real pain, he was leaning back, frowning. He felt as though someone was staring at him. As he looked up, he saw a transient, a bag lady, walking toward him. He suddenly felt very uneasy. She smiled and said, 'You're in a lot of pain, aren't you?'

"Feeling relieved, he mumbled, 'Yes, I was in an accident. I think my nose is broken.'

"'That's okay, THIS, TOO, SHALL PASS,' she stated calmly. Then she walked away. It was such an odd and unexpected thing to say it caught him off guard. He thought about it for quite a while and finally concluded she was right. The pain was temporary. He counted his blessings and felt better.

"Six weeks later, the same man was in the same hospital but for a very different reason. His first child was born. He was walking around handing out cigars. He stopped dead in his tracks when her saw her—The same bag lady that had helped him earlier. She smiled again and said, 'You're very happy, aren't you?'

"'Yes,' he replied enthusiastically. 'A baby boy, nine pounds six ounces. Mom was fine.'

"'Congratulations. THIS, TOO, SHALL PASS.'

"Len and I endured a great deal of adversity in our forty years of marriage. Despite all the challenges, pain, frustration and heartbreak, we always survived. When life would throw a new challenge our way, after the tears, fears and uncertainty passed, we would sit down and talk it through. It was almost always on paper, and solution based. We found that writing down our worries, concerns and fears always put things in perspective. One day, when our financial burdens were pressing down on us particularly hard, Len shared a quote he had read in a novel: *It's not how hard or far you fall, it's how high you bounce that counts. I smiled and added, a bend in the road is not the end of the road and falling is not failing.*

"As silly as it sounds, we would volley these little aphorisms and proverbs back and forth over the years. They became a part of us. We collected them like boys collect baseball cards and we taught them to our kids. We tried our best to live the ones we really believed. It wasn't always easy. We had been married about ten years when I found out I had cancer and things started looking particularly grim. We were reading everything we could find on people that had successfully recovered from that terrible disease. It's been so long now, I had almost forgotten. We had cried and talked through the night when Len said to me, 'I will always be here, no matter what. You never have to go this alone. I think this is a test from God! It's easy to trust God when things are going well. The real test of faith is if we trust God when things are going poorly.'

"Through all the surgery, the visits to the doctor and the sleepless nights, we continued to talk and plan. We resolved that we could and would get through this as we had so many other winters. There are many kinds of winters—financial, emotional, physical, spiritual. Len's passing is yet another winter to live through. He would have wanted us all to rejoice in life, not death. In his will he asked me to read this aloud in the event he passed before me. It's from a poem by John Donne. In the 1600s, in England, when someone would pass away, they would ring the church bell. Usually, a young boy was sent to find out who had died. John Donne's poem has real significance in the big picture...

No man is an island, entire of itself; every man is a piece of the continent, a part of the main; if a clod be washed away by the sea, Europe is the less, as well as if a promontory were, as well as if a manor of thy friends or of thine own were; any man's death diminishes me, because I am involved in mankind; and therefore never send to know for whom the bell tolls; it tolls for thee.

"We learned over the years to ask ourselves this simple question when something seemingly terrible happened: 'How do we know it's bad?' Time has a way of revealing profound lessons. We must remain aware and mindful as we wait to learn life's lessons. Challenges don't make the man, they reveal him to himself."

As Len's wife stepped down, I was wiping yet another tear from my cheek. "How strong she is," I thought silently to myself.

As I reflect on all the sad and horrifying things that have happened to my wife and I over the last twenty years, I smiled remembering what Len said to me one day. "The same rain that falls on your head, falls on us all eventually. Grieve. Feel the pain and sorrow. It's okay, however, it need not have a hold on us if we choose not to let it. At some point, we must move on."

Len's Lessons
Journal entries — *Releasing Resilience*

"The same rain that falls on your head falls on us all eventually. I carry my weather inside me."

"This, too, shall pass."

"It's not how far you fall, it's how high you bounce that counts. A bend in the road is not the end of the road and falling isn't failing. Get back on that horse."

"It's easy to trust God when things are going well. The real test is if you trust him when things are going poorly!"

"You never have to go it alone."

"It's okay to go to Hell, you just don't have to stay."

"Challenges don't make the man, they reveal him to himself."

"How do you know it's bad?"

Chapter 10
"Mutually Meaningful"

Len's best friend, Paul, stepped up to the podium. He was a learned man, well dressed, articulate and confident. He spoke with authority:

"For 60,000 years, the Australian Aboriginals have lived the following credo with little conflict. It is important to note that western conditions like ulcers, hypertension, cardiovascular disease and distress are conspicuously absent from their culture. They believe:

"We are only visitors. All encounters and experiences are 'forever connections.' We strive to close the circle of each experience. We do not leave frayed ends. If you walk away with bad feelings in your heart for another person, and that circle is not closed, it will repeat later on in your life. You will not suffer once, but over and over until you learn this simple truth. It is good to observe, learn and become wiser from what happened. It is good to give thanks and walk away in peace. We are never too old for worth."

Paul continued. "I called Len one day to complain about someone I had a conflict with. He said to me, 'Life and business are filled with conflict, it's unavoidable.'

"The dictionary defines conflict as *a collision or disagreement, a controversy or quarrel, a clash, a battle or struggle—especially a prolonged struggle.* The word immediately conjures something serious and intense. Conflict or disagreement is not inherently bad or good. Conflict is natural, normal, neutral and sometimes enlightening. It can turn into painful or disastrous ends, but it doesn't need to. How each of us views, approaches, and works through conflict does, to a large extent, determine our degree of success in the marketplace, in the family and in life. Miscommunication frequently occurs because of the numerous differences that exist between us. Ghandi said it eloquently: 'Each of us thinks our watch is telling the right time.'"

"Anyway, after I had told Len the details of the situation, he remarked that the cause was very similar to the last conflict I had told him about. In his customary way, he told me a true story...

"'A farmer in Eastern Washington walked into his bank in an old straw hat and dirty coveralls and made a transaction on a busy Friday afternoon. As he walked out to his truck, he remembered that he hadn't validated his parking ticket. He went back in and once again stood patiently in line. Twenty minutes later, he politely asked the same teller to validate his parking, a whopping sixty cent credit! The teller assumed some things about the farmer based on some very poor measures. She judged him by his clothes and by his easy going manner. She further assumed he was trying to pull one over on her, and looking down on him, refused the request, citing policy and procedure. He restated he had made a transaction twenty minutes earlier, with *her!* At this point, she became very short with him, refused again and asked him to either make a transaction or leave. There was a very long line behind him. He paused for a moment and asked her if she was sure about that. She said she was positive. He then contacted the branch manager and calmly restated his dilemma, hoping for an understanding ear and some action. The manager appeared indifferent and weakly said he would see what he could do. The gentle farmer replied he would wait for his phone call. The call never came. The next day he walked into the bank and promptly asked for a withdrawal slip. He proceeded to take exactly half of his savings, a little more than one million dollars, out of his account and proceeded to deposit it across the street at the bank's top competitor. Shocked and embarrassed, there was nothing the manager could do after the fact. Assuming and judging, in this case, cost that bank a substantial amount of long term profit and financial choices and flexibility.'"

"Len, satisfied with his story, leaned back in his chair

and smiled. 'There is a definite opportunity cost at stake. If you choose the way of conflict, it is at the cost of a great many other things. If you choose conflict, you are at once, choosing resentment, frustration, withholding, bitterness, anger, and lack of productivity. These negative emotions take their toll and come out in the form of stress, distress, lost revenue and strained relationships. There are many negative choices when dealing with conflict. My hope is, that after thoughtful consideration and reflection, you choose the healthiest and most productive option, a *Mutually Meaningful Solution... or The Win/Win Way.'*

"Len paused for a moment, then continued, 'Whenever each of us makes a decision to grow in any direction for good, there are always obstacles. This is certainly true with communication. At the heart of this curriculum is a fervent desire on my part for you to embrace this concept: *you don't need to be sick to get better.* Growth implies risk. It means trying and failing. It means getting out of our comfort zones temporarily. It means experimenting with new ideas that are a little scary because they are unfamiliar. It means letting go of the known and embracing the unknown for a little while. It means looking at situations and people with a new set of glasses. Not a Pollyanna, rose colored glasses, naïve view, but an honest, courageous, direct and assertive viewpoint and philosophy, the Win/Win Way.'

"'Where did you learn this, Len?' I interrupted.

"'Where else but in one of my favorite books, Lucy Beale's out of print masterpiece, *The Win/Win Way*. You see Paul,' he continued, 'conflict is a choice. Choosing collaboration is really choosing the Win/Win Way. This choice is more than strategy, it's choosing a new way of life, a whole new philosophy: *how can we both win?* It begins with the desire to find a solution. Sometimes it's a third or fourth option neither of us have considered. There is always another way. Like any other emotional state, effectively dealing with conflict in healthy ways is a choice.' Pausing for a moment and looking skyward, he continued. 'Paul, when I focus on the problem, it gets bigger. When I focus on the solution, it increases.'

"Here are some simple conflict-avoidance strategies that I learned from Len...

Active Listening

Listening builds trust quickly. Try the following the next time you're in a situation where someone is upset:

Listen Intently. Listen as if your life depends on it. Lean forward. Observe and take note of body language and extra verbal tones.

Pause three to five seconds before responding. It's hard, but with practice you'll be amazed at what you learn. People love to talk. Let them.

Question for clarification. Ask, 'How do you mean?' or, 'Can you give me an example?'

Paraphrase for understanding. Repeat, in one or two sentences, the main point of the speaker. When you hear the word 'Exactly!' you have true understanding. Occasionally, paraphrase the *emotions* you hear."

At this point, as I sat in the church, it occurred to me that Paul was giving a seminar. I looked around and people where smiling, taking notes, thoroughly engaged.

It's exactly what Len would have wanted.

Paul continued his talk. "The next thing I learned was...

Admit When You Are Wrong

If you have never developed this as a habit, it might be a little tough at first. A couple of years ago, I was having an early dinner with Len at a Thai restaurant downtown. I had parked in one of those 'No Parking between 4:00 p.m. and 6:00 p.m.' zones. I read the sign at about 3:10 p.m. and thought, 'I'll remember.' Riiiiiight! My back was to the window, although the car was right out front. About 4:30, Len said to me, 'Hey, Paul, isn't that your Bronco?' Turning around, what I saw made my heart leap into my mouth. I yelled, 'Yes!!!,' and jumped up to give chase. I was sprinting up the street, praying for a red light.

Fortunately, the light turned red as I approached the tow truck. I motioned to the scowling driver to roll down his window. He hesitated, then cautiously and slowly opened it about two inches. Somewhat out of breath, I remarked, 'I must have really screwed up somehow, because you have my car and I don't. Can we talk?' By this time, Len had caught up to us and was listening to my conversation with this pistol packing, burly, bearded tow truck driver. I proceeded to reaffirm my mistake and humbly asked him to consider options other than continuing on to his 'Barbed wire fenced, cost you $300 just to walk inside' wrecking yard. In this negotiation, if the outcome was to be *Mutually Meaningful*, I would have to utilize all of my people skills. He proceeded to tell me, 'If you had been rude to me or the slightest bit arrogant, I would have made you run for a while. It's a little test I like to give. You were nice about it. And since you continued to be decent, I've decided to cut you some slack.' I then proceeded to affirm to him how interesting and challenging his job must be, and he opened up like a dry flower to rain. He recounted story after humorous story of his towing trials and tribulations.

When the car was finally down off his tow truck, he said to me in a warm and jovial tone, 'You know, between the ticket from the city and the towing and storing charges, you would have paid over 400 bucks; but because you're a nice guy and not a jerk, you saved yourself $350 bucks. I'm going to ask you just to cover the hour I spent so I don't get in trouble at the office. $50 bucks and we'll call it square'

Len about fell over, composed himself, and said, 'Paul, let me get this,' and wrote a check to our bearded tow truck driving friend. He said to me later, 'that was one of the most valuable people lessons I have ever learned! Because I didn't have to suffer through it, I received a vicarious pleasure from it. It was worth way more than fifty dollars to me. Thanks!'

Afterward, Len summarized the main points, stressing to me why I was able to get my car back:

- You made him feel important tonight.

- You took the time to appreciate his positive qualities.

- You were genuinely interested in him and his work.

- You admitted you were wrong, quickly and vehemently.

- You employed Active Listening skills with dramatic results.

- You asked him to consider other options in a kind and courteous manner.

   "One of Len's gifts was his ability to...

Make The Other Person Feel Important

One of the ways to do this is to remember and use people's names in conversation. Want to shock and amaze someone that you just met? Remember their name the next time you see him or her. The effect is nothing short of amazing. It's esteeming to have someone respect you in that way. Here is a simple formula: Just remember *I.R.A.*

Imprint. Imprint their name into your sub-conscious by saying it quietly to yourself five or six times after you learn it. Then, in conversation, say it once or twice and always just before you leave as you are shaking their hand goodbye.

Repetition. Repeat it over and over again once you are alone. Consider writing it down in a journal or diary.

Association. Associate it with another person you know with that same name.

"One of the greatest leaders this country ever produced was Teddy Roosevelt. When he was a colonel in the Spanish American War, he memorized all 1,000 names of his famous Rough Riders. Many of them remained fiercely loyal to him, gladly helping in his campaigns for both Governor of New York and in his re-election to the Presidency in 1904.

Be Courteous And Kind To Everyone

We have a little poem on a plaque on the wall in our home that reads, *Hearts and minds open with little ease, with Thank You and If You Please.* Being courteous does not require any extra effort or great skill. It does take, however, a conscious and persistent effort until it becomes habitual.

Show Sincere Appreciation For Other People

Everyone wants to be appreciated and to be recognized for his or her accomplishments, strengths, skills or personhood. William James, the great educator, psychologist and author said, 'The deepest craving of any human being is to be appreciated.' He didn't say need, he said *craving!*

Become Genuinely Interested In Other People

You can make more friends in two hours by becoming genuinely interested in other people than you can in two weeks trying to get them interested in you. One of the secrets of Teddy Roosevelt's unprecedented popularity was his habit of discovering the interests of the person with whom he was to meet the next day. He would stay up late the night before reading up on that person's passionate interest. Wow, is it any wonder he was so well liked?

Speak In Terms Of Your Own Feelings First

Be assertive when a situation or person has you frustrated or angry. Begin in a friendly way, using 'I'-Statements such as, 'At this moment, I am feeling frustrated at the situation because...,' or 'I am confused, can you help me to understand?' 'I'-Statements contain no blame or judgement. What is conspicuously missing from 'I'-Statements is the word YOU.

"If you develop the habit of combining the use of 'I' statements with 'Active Listening,' they form a powerful duo in achieving effective communication by providing clarity and keeping the communication flow open.

Don't Argue Or Tell Another Person They're wrong

Ben Franklin was a master of this. He was not, however, always good at tact and diplomacy. An older Quaker friend of his one day rebuked him and strongly suggested he change his argumentative ways or it would be the end of his business career in Philadelphia. To Franklin's credit, at age 28, he sat down and created a plan to change. He resolved never to argue or criticize from that day forward. This is what he would say instead: 'It appears to me at this time...' or 'I apprehend it to be...,' 'I could be wrong, I frequently am, however, it seems to me at present...' In his 70s, the great inventor and writer was asked to be the overseas diplomat to both England and France.

Ask Questions Instead Of Giving Orders, Advice Or Opinion

Questions like, "Would you be so kind as to..." or "If you wouldn't mind, could you...?" or "How do you feel about...?" These subtle approaches have tremendous influence, and yet inspire others to think the idea is theirs. Once they do believe the idea is their own, let them go on believing so. If you think about it, what difference does it make, really? Do you want cooperation and results or to temporarily gratify your ego?"

Paul had talked longer than anyone else, yet I never once sensed anyone was offended. It was as though Len was up there. He continued, "As a bright, promising young man in India, Ghandi's first profession was law. He was an attorney. He was anxious to do well on his first case. As he began to dig into the case he realized it was possible to settle the dispute amicably and without going to court. He ended up drafting a *Mutually Meaningful* solution. Everyone won except the law firm. He was fired from that company. It was a turning point in his career.

"Relationships, harmonious and respectful in nature," Paul concluded, "will ennoble an environment that fosters trust, competence, interdependence and outstanding results. None of us succeed alone. Each of us needs the cooperation of others, with a minimum of conflict. I have a poem in my office Len gave me that simply states, *Only one life that soon is past. Only what's done with love will last.* I am convinced that the quality of my life is directly related to the quality of all my relationships. I can ill-afford to have even one strained relationship in my life if I am to complete the race I am running. We can play the victim or get up and do something about our skills, knowledge and attitudes that hold us back from harmonious relationships with others. Some conflicts can never be averted; however, with repetition and an expanded awareness, we may resolve sooner those that might escalate into something we'll later regret. Isn't it worth a try? What have we got to lose, except for some excess baggage and grief. That is the legacy Len left for me. Thanks for being here to honor him."

As Paul left the podium, I was sad that he stopped talking. I grabbed my journal and captured the following:

Len's Lessons
Mutually Meaningful

"Active Listening builds trust and is always worth the effort."

"Always admit when you are wrong, it's what BIG people do."

"Make other people feel important."

"Stay away from arguments and resist the urge to tell someone they are wrong."

"Avoid speaking in the second person which is, in effect, 'Shoulding' on someone. Avoid giving unsolicited advice or opinions."

"There is always another way. The third alternative in any conflict is usually Mutually Meaningful but takes time and effort to create."

Chapter 11
"Analyze Associations"

"Get around people** who have something of value to share with you. Their impact will continue to have a significant impact on your life long after they have departed." That was Len. The things he taught me continue to come back to me like a beautiful sunset after several cloudy days. I forget at times how much I learned from him that I have taken for granted. They have become a part of me, his legacy and wisdom will never die. I have done my best to pass on what I learned from him. I will spend the rest of my life sharing what I have learned with others who are ready to hear, ready to learn, ready to grow, ready to change for the better.

"Never underestimate the power of association. You'll be the same person in five years with the exception of two things: the people you associate with and the books that you read. Who are you hanging around with, and why? Is it okay? Never underestimate the power of association. Choose your friends and mentors with great care.

They will assist you in your ascent or drag you down to the depths of hell. From experience I can tell you this is true."

The speaker was Len's business partner, Bob. Bob had been to hell and back and had the scars to prove it. "It's easy to get nudged off course. It's easy to become complacent and not pay attention to the voices that will influence you. Negative change is subtle. Bad habits are easy to form and hard to live with. Good habits are hard to form but easy to live with. Mentors, coaches, the right coaches, will stretch you and force you to grow in areas that will make you uncomfortable. You will feel uneasy, out of your comfort zone for a while. That kind of pain is good, it pushes you.

"Avoid the easy crowd. Hang around the people who have high expectations of you, the kind of people who will hold you accountable for your actions and decisions and keep you on track. Len was that kind of person. He would never let you slack off unless it was planned. Work hard, play hard, he used to say. *Relax on purpose. Make sure you have something to look forward to. All work and no play make Jack a dull boy.*"

Bob smiled as he reminisced about how he and Len met. "A mutual friend of ours introduced us. Jack was a character. He had a knack for putting people together. Bob and Len was a match made in heaven. Lennon and

McCartney, Rogers and Hammerstein, Laurel and Hardy, Martin and Lewis, Peanut Butter and Jelly, we were each other's alter ego. Our friend Jack seemed to know that. It was uncanny the day he introduced us. He just seemed to know a fit would exist.

"From our first meeting, I knew we would find a way to work together. Len was a natural salesman. He loved people. I preferred to work behind the scenes. The financials, the details, the followup, those were the things I enjoyed and was good at. Len hated details but loved people. He loved the thrill of the hunt, closing the deal. He lived for that. Once the deal was done, he handed over the details and the operational aspect to me. You know, he had a big heart. He had a sixth sense about people who were in pain and yet were ready to change. He just knew.

"Over time, I began to meet some of you. Len would bring you into the office. He would take enormous amounts of time to help someone if he felt they were ready to change. *If you take one step, I'll take two.* I must have heard him say that a hundred times if I heard it once. Len was a farmer. He grew people. He grew them right where they were. He was a teacher, a coach. He would teach them from where they were, not from where he was. He would give you just enough to stretch you but never overwhelm you. Drop by drop, bit by bit you would learn. He was always trying to work himself out of a job.

"When Len was eight years old, he had a Huffy bicycle, with the banana seat and the butterfly handle bars. He taught himself to ride with training wheels. His best friend was a year younger. He approached Len and asked him to teach him how to ride a bike without training wheels. The other kids were making fun of him. He was ready.

"'Okay,' Len said, 'you've got to pay attention, focus. You need to trust me, I'll be with you all the way. Fair enough?'

"'Yes,' his friend said, 'I trust you. Let's do it.'

"Len ran behind his friend with encouraging words and enthusiasm. 'You're getting it, great job, keep it going.' Then it happened, off he went on his own. As he went around the block, Len had the tremendous feeling that only comes of giving, of helping, of teaching.

"Once his friend came around again, Len's role changed to one of part time coach. It did not require as much time. As his friend went by, he would yell, "Eyes straight ahead, pedal fast. You're doing great!" I think that was how Len was able to help so many people: after time his role changed. Eventually, he worked himself out of a job. That magic moment when the student grasps the concept, the skill, the success. Few things in life are more rewarding than that special moment.

"Len's mother told me that story. She said, just before she died, that at that moment, teaching his friend how to ride a bike, he had found his moment in the sun, his bliss. Most people never do find that bliss. Len was a teacher, a coach. He loved people. He helped a lot of people. Many of them are here today. He would have loved this. As humble as he was, he loved a good party. This isn't a funeral, it's a celebration of life. Thank you all for coming."

That was Bob. Brief. As he walked away from the podium I reflected back on a conversation Len and I once had: "Successful people are like the prettiest girl in High School. She never has a date on Friday night because all the guys are too afraid to ask her out. Fear of rejection. If they only knew she hadn't had a date in six months because of fear. Successful men and women are more than happy to help those who have the courage to ask for help. I have never had any BIG person refuse request for help. Help with direction. Help with guidance. Help with books. Help with associations."

Smiling, Len went on. "Remember, when you leave this earth, you take nothing with you that you have received—only what you have given. A full heart, enriched by honest service to others; love, sacrifice and courage." Emerson wrote, If we are related, we shall meet. The law of attraction is immutable. The best of all things is to learn. Money can be lost or stolen, health can fail, but what you commit to your mind is yours forever.

Successful people will help you if you ask. I believe it's because they see a little of themselves in you and feel a responsibility to help usually because someone helped them. Common threads in BIG people begin to appear after a while. Things like *Gratitude, Courage, Caring, Faith, Resilience, Curiosity, Compassion, Integrity, Industry, Creativity, and Loyalty."*

It wasn't until years later I realized how deep Len's well was or how he was able to dig it so deep. People and Books, the two great influences on his life. Now, as I look around the Church, I see the tremendous legacy he left. It is an extraordinary 'shade Tree'. Lives he touched, people he had helped.

Len said to me near the end of his life, "Who are you hanging around and why? Is it okay? Give that some serious thought and then, if it makes sense, make the necessary changes in your associations. In the long run, you'll be glad you did."

Len's Lessons
Analyze Associations

"Never underestimate the power of Association."

"You are the same today as you'll be in five years except for two things: the people you meet and the books you read."

"If we are related, we shall meet."

"Who are you hanging around and why? Is it okay?"

Chapter 12
"Wanting Worthwhile Work"

What drove Len? Why did he work so willingly for others the way he did? A week before he died, my very last time with my mentor and coach, I asked him this question. He paused for what seemed like an eternity… then replied in a slow and very deliberate manner, "Let me tell you a story," taking his glasses off for effect.

"I was thirteen years old and we were vacationing at a lake one hot August week. I was with my best friend, Tommy. His family had a cabin on Lake Entiat. That lake was, and is, the best water skiing in the state.

Tommy and I had taken the boat out early, 5:15 in the morning. There was not another boat in site. This particular action went against our better judgment and broke all the rules of common sense. We both knew it was wrong, but when you're thirteen, you mistakenly believe you'll live forever.

"While everyone else was asleep, we pushed the boat out by hand and drifted down the lake with the silent paddle of an Indian Brave. Another mile, and we fired up the engines. It was amazing. We knew it was wrong, but forbidden fruit does seem to taste sweeter. It was the most fun I've ever had water skiing. The lake was glass, like a mirror reflecting the brown hillsides and the crimson hue of the most magnificent sunrise I have ever witnessed. It just didn't get any better than this. It was the perfect morning.

"At that moment, Tommy and I had never been closer. He was my best friend. Tommy was the kind of guy that pushed everything to the limit. If you did twenty pushups, he did forty. If you ran one mile, he ran two, and would tease you all the way around the track. He had charm, charisma, and talent. Everyone loved him. His smile could charm a bird out of a tree. The guys wanted to be like him, the girls (and their mothers!) wanted to be with him. He would bring a single carnation over to the house and give it to my mom *every time* he came over. I used to think it was corny and strange, but my mother loved him for it. She would go on and on about him after he was gone. She never actually came out and said it but I could tell she hoped I would turn out as thoughtful as Tommy. I found out later he brought a carnation to the lady of every house he visited.

"By the time the sun had cleared the horizon, we had skied three exhausting runs. Tommy turned to me with that magic smile and the twinkle in his eye, and said,

'One more run buddy, for the road.'

"'I'm exhausted, let's go in,' I said. 'Your parents will be up soon and you know how your Dad will be if he finds out we went out alone. He feels pretty strongly about always having three in a boat,' I said tentatively. Tommy gave a Cheshire Cat grin, knowing full well I was right, but that devil-may-care attitude was one of the reasons he was so popular. The silence was deafening. He just stared, waiting for me to blink.

"'Oh, all right! I take one more short run,' I said, pretending I hated it. I hopped in the boat and said those two magic words of summer: 'Hit it!' As tired as I was, it was a great run. Tommy had taught me how to push the envelope and as I cut across the wake back and forth I remember thinking, *This is it. It doesn't get any better. If I died right now I'd be happy.* I let go of the rope, drifted to a stop and leaned back with the morning sun on my face, the icy water all around, blissful.

"A searing pain ran through my quadriceps, the cramp of all cramps. I'd had them before, but this one was a doozy. I doubled over in pain and panicked, kicking off my skis. For some inexplicable reason, I was not wearing my life vest. Tom saw my predicament and hurriedly turned the boat around. When he made the first pass, I had actually gone under the water. I couldn't swim—the pain had incapacitated me. With the boat running in a gentle forward idle, Tommy dove in the water. By the time he got to me, I had gone under a third time. As I was sinking, I felt a strong hand grab mine and pull me up.

"We must have been fifteen feet under water, yet he somehow pulled me out. Neither of us were aware that the boat was still circling around us. Tommy attempted to calm me with reassuring words, but I couldn't shake off the pain. At the very moment I knew I was going to be okay, the boat came around and hit Tommy full in the back of the head. His hands slipped away from my chest, and he sank rapidly into the lake. The scene was in slow motion. He was unconscious and I was helpless. I reached for him and missed. My heart sank. The pain in my leg did not allow me to go after him as he had for me. In an instant he was gone.

The reality of what had happened did not hit me until hours later. I was in shock. His parents were hysterical and overwhelmed with grief. His mother wept and cried like I had never heard, yet she never once blamed me or delivered a harsh or critical word.

"Tommy was the oldest boy in a family of five, four girls and he. Tommy had been the one child to whom his father had given his unrestricted warmth and deepest love; in return, he had been the perfect model child for the others, always reliable, always hard-working, always respectful. But now he was dead, and all that his father could do was grieve and pray.

Three months later, Tommy's father asked me to meet him for lunch. It was a somber and serious two hours. Yet, despite the grief, we reminisced about all the great times we both had had with Tommy. At the end of the meal, he slid Tommy's journal to me and said, "You were his best friend. I think you should have this, he would have wanted you to."

"Afterward, we took a long drive back to the lake. Tommy's family and I said our final goodbye to him that day. The most powerful thing I have ever witnessed was his four sisters and mother crying one last time, tossing a single carnation into the lake, and bowing their heads in prayer. Christina, Tommy's youngest sister, said, 'set the table, Tommy, and wait for us. We'll see you up there for dinner before you know it!' We all wept. Finally, his father said, 'Let's recall one great thing about Tommy that we cherish most in our hearts.' A small boat bearing a lantern was pushed out onto the lake. That ritual, symbolic and powerful, was the last goodbye, a final farewell, closure to the grief and suffering.

"At that moment, I made a promise to myself that I would live two lives: the one I had planned for myself, and one of service to others for Tommy. The Bible says, *Greater love hath no man than that he would give his life for his brother.* I promised Tommy that day that I would help others every day without complaint or delay. I owed him that. I have done my best ever since to honor that promise."

As Len wiped away the tears, he concluded, "I have never told anyone that story. Now you know what drives me. Here is a letter Tommy wrote to himself. It's from his journal. I want you to have it. It's the most precious thing I own. Now it's yours. Keep it going."

Carpe Diem

I want to seize every day that is given to me. I believe each day is a gift from "The Sweet Hereafter." I pledge to make the most of every day I have, because you just never know. I want to learn and work and play as if I'll live forever and live as if I'll die tomorrow. Today is a good day to die. I don't want to die, I love life and it's been great to me so far. I have so many plans, so many things to see, do, share, have and become. I can't wait to be able to realize some of those things, but I also recognize I have to live just for today.

I want to help a lot of people. I want to make a difference in people's lives. Most people can't seem to get out of their own way. I believe everyone feels sorry for themselves and a lot of people are lonely or afraid. I want to help them see that we don't have to live that way. If I can get rid of the FEAR that holds me back, I know I can do amazing things. From today forward, I vow to live without FEAR. I will take risks, jump in the water instead of sitting in the boat, and get it done. I'll do something today that I don't want to do, just for the exercise. I will read something meaningful and force my mind to stretch. I will be happy. I will count my blessings instead of my setbacks. I will not be afraid. I'll take the time to smell the roses.

I will be a friend. I'll find something nice to say about someone, little things that matter to that person. I'll try to see things from another person's point of view. I'll keep working and reaching for the things I want and be of service to others. I figure I can have whatever I want if I just help enough other people get what they want first. And finally, I'll make the time every day to give thanks for all I have. I know I'm blessed. It's a great life.

Tommy

I wept like a baby. So that was it. Two lives. He lived one for Len and one for Tommy. Now I know.

Epilogue

Freedom from Fear is more important than freedom from want! Len taught me how to live that principle. His method was very unusual, at least to me. I'll never forget what he said to me that first day: "I will help you on two conditions: first, you can't tell anyone I helped you until after I'm no longer around. Second, once you are back on your feet, you must at some point give this gift away to others. Fair enough?"

I looked at him for what seemed like an eternity wondering why he would insist on such a strange understanding. What was in it for him? I finally stammered out a reply. "Sure."

You see, I was teachable, ready. I had hit a bottom of sorts. "I will make the time to share my philosophy with you, teach you to ride a bike without training wheels until you can ride on your own," he said. "At that point, our relationship will change. My job with you is to work myself out of a job. Fair enough?"

Over the next five years, Len invested his time, energy and wisdom to share his unique philosophy with me. He never once asked anything in return. He consistently affirmed my progress, praising my every advance. He would say, "I'm proud of you, thanks for helping me." Helping *him*? I was doing all the taking. I could live to be 120 and not be able to pay him back. So now my journey lies in trying to give away to others who are ready the same things that Len so generously gave to me. I'm up to the task. Thanks, Len.

*It's about what I like to call 'Enlightened Self Interest.' That is, the combination of Charity, Moral Obligation and Righteousness that demands **giving** on several levels. The first level is simply to help another help himself. Coaching. You know, teach him how to fish, you feed him for a lifetime. The next is to help someone who cannot possibly help you in return. The highest form of this giving is to combine the two and add an additional and difficult element. It is the most noble and yet at the same time, the most rewarding and results in a power-filled state for the giver; that is, to help someone anonymously, in secret, with clear conditions that no one must know. It requires a dying of self. A letting go of ego gratification. It's LOVE in its purest form. It's self-discipline combined with a daily dying of self until it becomes a habit and, eventually, a lifestyle. It takes a lifetime to master, yet it is the most rewarding work on earth.*

Finally, add to this the ongoing commitment to elimi-

nate FEAR and all its various forms to lead the life imag-
ined. I now believe it means that anything we can do to
eliminate FEAR, that great destroyer of dreams, will bring
us happiness and joy for a lifetime.

As we solemnly walked out of that old church, a rain-
bow appeared. I said a prayer of thanks to have been fortunate enough to have met a man so special, a man who
had touched so many lives for good. I would do my best
to carry the torch.

About the Author

Mark Matteson is President of Pinnacle Service Group. Mark is in demand nationally as an inspirational and "Edutaining" Keynote Speaker, Seminar Leader and Writer on topics such as Sales, Customer Service, Productivity and Morale, Management, Leadership, Employee Attraction and Retention. A gifted storyteller, he uses Humor to make powerful points that positively affect the bottom line. As an Outcome based consultant, he develops collaborative relationships with business leaders that result in a direct contribution to the client's profitability.

Mr. Matteson works with Organizations around the country to raise the bar in their personal and professional performance.

Call Mark today for your next industry gathering or Organizational Change effort. He can be reached toll free at 206-697-0454, or online at www.SparkingSuccess.net.